What's in this book

This book belongs to

_____

暑假来了！
The summer holidays are here!

学习内容 Contents

沟通 Communication

说说休闲活动
Talk about leisure
activities

生词 New words

★	带	to bring
★	床	bed
★	网球	tennis, tennis ball
★	河	river
★	先	first
★	骑马	to ride a horse
★	然后	then, next
★	回家	to go home
	暑假	summer holidays
	捉	to catch
	房间	room
	睡觉	to sleep
	希望	to hope

第三天，他们先去骑马，然后去爬山。
The third day, they went horse riding first, and then they went climbing.

文化 Cultures

中国的传统游戏
Traditional Chinese games

跨学科学习 Project

了解电影放映原理，并制作一本
手翻书
Learn how a film works and make
a flip book

Get ready

1 What did you do during the last summer holidays?

2 What do you want to do for the next summer holidays?

3 Where do you think Hao Hao is?

Summer holidays
1 July

shǔ jià
暑假

dài
带

暑假来了，伊森和艾文带浩浩去他们的爷爷奶奶家里玩。

4

"浩浩，别躺在床上了，起来打网球吧！"第二天早上，艾文说。

河 hé

捉 zhuō

下午，爷爷带着他们去河里捉鱼。
浩浩捉了一条大鱼。

晚上，他们回到房间，伊森说："赶快睡觉吧。明天的活动更好玩。"

xiān
先

rán hòu
然后

qí mǎ
骑马

第三天，他们先去骑马，然后去爬
山。浩浩玩得很开心。

离开的时候，浩浩说："真不想回家，希望明年暑假能再来！"

Let's think

1 Recall the story. Put the correct activities in order and write the letters.

a

b

c

d

e

f

⬜ ➡️ ⬜ ➡️ ⬜ ➡️ ⬜

2 If you were a friend of Ethan and Ivan, would you like to spend your summer holidays at their grandparents' place in the countryside? Discuss with your friend.

我想去他们的爷爷奶奶家，因为我喜欢大自然 / ……

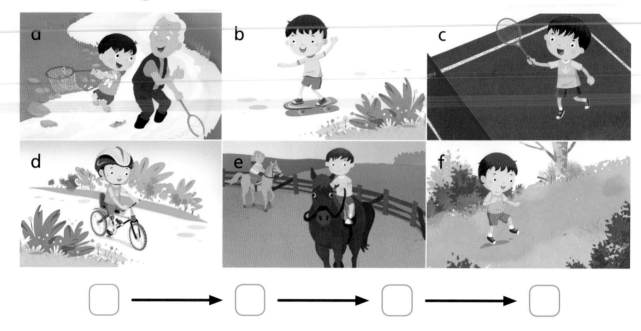

在那儿，我可以吃……

我可以……

我不想去那里，因为城市里更方便。

城市里有很多商店，我喜欢……

我可以去……

New words

02 | 1 | Learn the new words.

Happy summer holidays!
暑假

① 先
骑马

② 然后
捉
河
带

③ 网球

④ 睡觉
床
房间

暑假来了，
我希望……

回家

2 Work with your friend. Say the words in the pictures and ask your friend to point to them.

听听说说 Listen and say

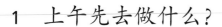

1 Listen and circle the correct pictures.

2 Look at the pictures. Listen to the story a

1 上午先去做什么？

①

🧑‍🦰 小朋友，你们好！这里有很多好
玩的活动。我带你们看看。

2 在公园里可以做
什么？

③

3 明天几点要坐车
回家？

👧 浩浩，前面有河！

👦 知道了！跳、跳、跳！

浩浩，你打网球吗？

我先骑马，然后打网球。

这里真好玩，我不想回家了！

我们都不想回家了！

1

你想去哪里？

我想先……，然后……

2

她要买……

……先……，然后……

3

它要……

……

Task

Look at the flyer for a class outing. Think of other activities and design a flyer of your own. Then talk about it with your friend.

4月18日
上午
9:00

11:30

下午
2:30

3:30

四月十八日，我们去公园玩。上午，我们先画画，然后吃饭。下午，……

Game

Choose two words, make a sentence and ask your friends to do the actions.

骑马

跑

衣服

饭

刷牙

画画

自行车

面条

汤

唱歌

巧克力

网球

跳

看电视

我们先骑马，然后回家吃饭。

Chant

 Listen and say.

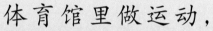

暑假来了，暑假来了，
从早到晚活动多。
星期一，先骑马，
然后打网球。
星期二，你唱歌，
我们来跳舞。
体育馆里做运动，
电影院里看电影。
暑假生活真快乐，
希望天天是暑假！

生活用语 Daily expressions

好玩儿！
This is fun!

好听！
This (The music) is good!

写一写 Write

1 Trace and write the characters.

ノ ク タ タ タ タ 妖 妖 然 然 然 然

一 厂 厂 斤 后 后

然 后 然 后

然 后

丨 冂 冂 冂 回 回

丶 宀 宀 宀 宇 宇 宇 家 家

回 家 回 家

回 家

2 Write and say.

放学了，我想先去图书馆，_____和妹妹一起_____。

3 Fill in the blanks with the correct words. Colour the drums using the same colours.

 然后

 回家

 打球

 时间

你星期六有_____吗？

星期六上午我和爸爸妈妈要出去。我们先去_____，_____去爷爷家吃饭。下午三点_____。你三点半来我家玩吧。

拼音输入法 Pinyin input

Create a paragraph. Choose appropriate letters for the blue, green and pink blanks and complete the yellow ones using your own ideas. Then type it and read it to your friend.

a 动物	f 看狮子	k 跑步
b 运动	g 吃糖果	l 和小狗玩
c 吃	h 游泳	m 餐馆
d 打功夫	i 画动物	n 公园
e 吃饼干	j 喝汤	o 动物园

我很喜欢___。星期六，我先___，然后___。星期日，我去了___。在那里，我先___，然后_____
_____。

Cultures

1 Learn about some traditional Chinese games.

别捉我！

Hawk-and-chicks:
A 'hawk' tries to catch the 'chicks', while a 'hen' protects her children who line up behind her.

我开始捉人了。

一、二、三，向前跳！

Hopscotch: Draw squares on the ground, throw a stone into a square, and then hop and jump along the squares to get the stone.

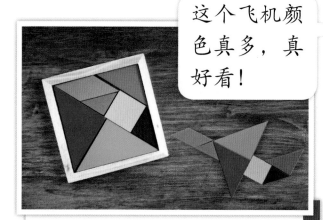

这个飞机颜色真多，真好看！

Tangram: A square cut into seven pieces. The pieces can be used to form different shapes.

2 Make your own tangram. Cut a piece of cardboard into seven pieces. Form different shapes and show them to your friend. Whose shapes are more interesting?

我先骑马，然后坐船。

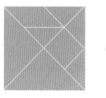 →

Project

1 Do you like watching films? Have you ever wondered how a film works? Go behind the scenes to see what makes the magic happen.

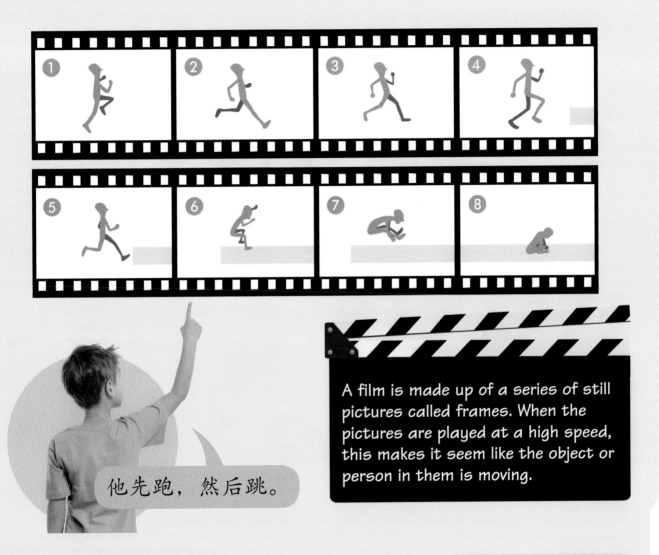

A film is made up of a series of still pictures called frames. When the pictures are played at a high speed, this makes it seem like the object or person in them is moving.

他先跑，然后跳。

2 Use what you have just learnt to create a flip book. Show it to your friend.

他先走，然后跑。

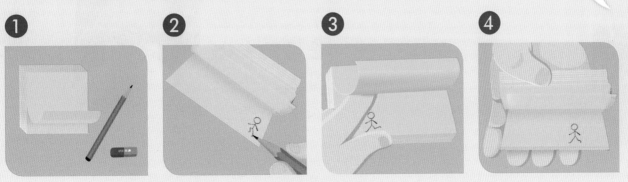

温习 Checkpoint

1 Play noughts and crosses with your friend. Complete the sentences or write the characters correctly before marking Os or Xs in the squares. The first player who has a row of three Os or Xs wins.

她能 …… 和 ……

爸爸妈妈 ……
我们去 …… 买
蔬菜和水果。

这只熊在 ……
里 …… 鱼。

我先吃面包，

写作业。

昨天爸爸在北京
工作，今天他

了！

今天我和爸
爸妈妈去公
园玩，……
不会下雨。

它不在床上……
它在树上……

弟弟在……
里……

8 a.m.

……她在……

2 Work with your friend. Colour the stars and the chillies.

Words and sentences	说	读	写
带	☆	☆	🌶
床	☆	☆	🌶
网球	☆	☆	🌶
河	☆	☆	🌶
先	☆	☆	🌶
骑马	☆	☆	🌶
然后	☆	☆	☆
回家	☆	☆	☆
暑假	☆	🌶	🌶
捉	☆	🌶	🌶
房间	☆	🌶	🌶
睡觉	☆	🌶	🌶
希望	☆	🌶	🌶
第二天，他们先去骑马，然后去爬山。	☆	🌶	🌶

Talk about leisure activities	☆

3 What does your teacher say?

21

分享 Sharing

Words I remember

带	dài	to bring
床	chuáng	bed
网球	wǎng qiú	tennis, tennis ball
河	hé	river
先	xiān	first
骑马	qí mǎ	to ride a horse
然后	rán hòu	then, next
回家	huí jiā	to go home
暑假	shǔ jià	summer holidays
捉	zhuō	to catch
房间	fáng jiān	room
睡觉	shuì jiào	to sleep
希望	xī wàng	to hope

Other words

躺	tǎng	to lie
起来	qǐ lái	to get up
赶快	gǎn kuài	immediately
好玩	hǎo wán	fun
爬山	pá shān	to climb a hill/mountain
开心	kāi xīn	happy
离开	lí kāi	to leave
时候	shí hòu	time, moment

OXFORD
UNIVERSITY PRESS

Oxford University Press is a department of the University of Oxford.
It furthers the University's objective of excellence in research, scholarship,
and education by publishing worldwide. Oxford is a registered trade mark of
Oxford University Press in the UK and in certain other countries

Published in Hong Kong by
Oxford University Press (China) Limited
39th Floor, One Kowloon, 1 Wang Yuen Street, Kowloon Bay,
Hong Kong

© Oxford University Press (China) Limited 2017

The moral rights of the author have been asserted

First Edition published in 2017

All rights reserved. No part of this publication may be reproduced, stored in a
retrieval system, or transmitted, in any form or by any means, without the prior
permission in writing of Oxford University Press (China) Limited, or as expressly
permitted by law, by licence, or under terms agreed with the appropriate
reprographics rights organization. Enquiries concerning reproduction outside
the scope of the above should be sent to the Rights Department, Oxford
University Press (China) Limited, at the address above

You must not circulate this work in any other form
and you must impose this same condition on any acquirer

Illustrated by Anne Lee, Emily Chan, KY Chan and Wildman

Photographs for reproduction permitted by Dreamstime.com

China National Publications Import & Export (Group) Corporation is an authorized distributor of
Oxford Elementary Chinese.

Please contact content@cnpiec.com.cn or 86-10-65856782

ISBN: 978-0-19-082313-9

10 9 8 7 6 5 4 3 2